PRESENTED TO

Scott Barrow

BY

Grandma and Grandpa Barrow

April 15, 1984

DATE

Whatsoever ye shall ask
in prayer,
believing,
ye shall receive.
Matthew 21:22

Book of
CHRISTIAN PRAYER

Leslie F. Brandt

AUGSBURG PUBLISHING HOUSE
Minneapolis, Minnesota

BOOK OF CHRISTIAN PRAYER

Copyright © 1980 Augsburg Publishing House

Library of Congress Catalog Card No. 73-88603

International Standard Book No. 0-8066-1751-9

Scripture quotations unless otherwise noted are from the Revised Standard Version of the Bible, copyright 1946, 1952, and 1971 by the Division of Christian Education of the National Council of Churches.

Prayers on pages 40, 44, 45, 47-56, 58, 59, 61, 64-66, 68-74, 126, 130-132, and 143 are adapted from *Growing Together,* copyright © 1975 by Augsburg Publishing House. Prayers on pages 154-159 are from *Psalms/Now* by Leslie F. Brandt © 1973 Concordia Publishing House. Used by permission.

MANUFACTURED IN THE UNITED STATES OF AMERICA

CONTENTS

FOR SPECIAL PEOPLE

MY RELATIONSHIP WITH GOD

SERVANTHOOD AND DISCIPLESHIP

PRAISE AND THANKS

GROWING OLDER

NATION AND WORLD

IN THE EVENING

CONTEMPORARY PSALMS

IN THE
MORNING

BLESS HIS NAME!

"Bless the Lord, O my soul;
and all that is within me, bless his holy name!"
It is thus, O God, that I want to begin this day—
blessing you, praising you, adoring you,
as did the ancient psalmist.
You have kept me through the night.
You have forgiven me the sins
and errors of yesterday.
Now I am privileged to begin a new day,
to start over again,
to step out into this world as your child and servant,
assigned to serve in your purposes.
I praise you with the assurance that,
as you watch over your own through the night,
so you will walk with us through each day.
I dedicate this day to you, O Lord,
that I may travel in that course you set before me.
Help me to be faithful and obedient
to the voice of your Spirit within me,
and allow my morning praises
to continue throughout this day,
reflecting your love and glory
in all my relationships and activities.

WHAT I WANT
FOR TODAY

You've granted me another day, O Lord.
Yesterday, with its wasted opportunities
and selfish enterprises, is gone forever.
I don't suppose today will be much different, Lord.
But it could be,
if I stay within your orbit for my life
and run your errands
and recognize my appointment and commitment
as your servant within this fractured world.
So be it, Lord.
It is what I want, Lord.
Because of me, or in spite of me,
may your love touch some lonely, needy person today.
I no longer want to build empires,
to ascend thrones,
or to be number one in my little kingdom.
I want to love you,
and to respond to your love for me
by communicating such love to others.
This is what I want, O Lord,
but you know my weaknesses;
may the victory today be yours.

WHEN THE WORLD LOOKS OMINOUS

The world looks ominous today, O Lord.
I am reluctant to leave my warm bed,
the security of my home,
to brave the elements of nature
and the distortions of this human race.
I don't feel that I have what it takes
to live as you would have me live
amid the pains and problems
of your people around me.
I am afraid, Lord, and I am ashamed.
Give me courage, O God.
You do not require that I win every battle.
You simply ask that I pick up my arms—
or my cross—
and enter into the arena of life.
You do not ask me to fret or fuss
over the insurmountable circumstances
that confront me.
You simply ask that I be myself—
your child, your disciple, your representative—
reaching out to others in love,
helping bear another's burdens,
allowing your Spirit to work out your will
through me.
So I go forth, my great God,
by your orders, and in your power.
Have it your way, O Lord, in me and through me.

THANKS FOR
ANOTHER DAY

Thank you, my loving God, for another day.
I don't know what adventures it holds for me.
I may be surprised by joy,
or wounded by pain or sorrow.
Help me to be thankful in all circumstances,
to believe that what comes my way
comes by way of your loving will and permission.
Grant, O God, that I meet it as your child,
without doubt or fear,
knowing that whatever happens,
my relationship to you is never in jeopardy.
And grant that I may be able
to bring your love and joy
into the difficult circumstances that confront me.

A PROBLEM
THAT PERSISTS

I've long had this problem, Lord,
this pernicious little demon
that keeps disturbing my peace of mind.
Maybe you permit it
to hover around the fringes of my life
to drive me incessantly to your fountain of grace.
More likely it is my own little pet.
I want to keep it out of sight
but not out of consciousness.
It may even be a part of my God-given morality
which I can't dislodge
until I am evicted from this body.
Keep it, O Lord,
from coming between me and you today,
and keep it from hurting my brothers and sisters.
And thank you, Lord,
for accepting and loving
and using me just as I am,
and for persisting in drawing me
toward what you want me to be.

THE BLESSING
OF SOLITUDE

I am alone, dear God,
alone to greet the sun or rain,
the clouds or blue skies of this day before me.
I am, for this day, apart from the crowd,
separated from friends and relatives,
alone with myself—and with you—
and I will, throughout this day,
hear no voice but my own.
But I need not, I will not be lonely.
I know that you are always with me.
I may even come to know you better,
to love you more,
in the precious solitude of this remarkable day.
Evidence of your creative power is all about me.
The sunrise and the sunset, the light and the darkness,
the heavens, the flowers,
the tall pine reaching out toward the sky—
all show forth your handiwork.
Away from city distractions,
I may even sense in some special way
your perpetual presence in the quietness and peace
of this blessed solitude.
And so I greet this day with joy and praise,
seeking enrichment so that I will be better able
to manifest you and your divine peace
among my sisters and brothers
when I return to the hustle of a blustery world.
God bless this day.

17

HELP ME
FACE TODAY

I should be grateful for a new day, Lord,
especially after a sleepless night.
But, God forgive me, I'm not.
There's something I must face today,
and it scares me even to think about it.
You have said that I need never be afraid
if I walk in your footsteps.
You have promised that all things
will work out for good for those who follow you.
You have challenged me to live
joyfully and thankfully,
whatever the circumstances that crowd me.
Help me to get my values in order, O God,
to measure my progress by your perspectives,
to gauge my success by your measurements.
O God, help me to trust you,
even if I appear to make no progress whatsoever
or fail in what I propose to do.
My life is yours, O Lord,
and so is this day before me.
I submit the coming hours into your hands
and pray that your Spirit may guide me
through this dark tunnel of doubt.
If it be your will,
enable me to break into the bright sunlight
of victory at the other end.

ANOTHER DAY
OF WAITING

O God, so much of life is wasted in waiting:
for a dear one to return home,
for a letter from a lover,
for news about a friend who is very ill,
for a paycheck to sustain my bodily needs.
The dawn of a new day is the dawn of another day
of marking time, hoping, longing, and aching.
Teach me, dear God, how to turn the days of waiting
into days of opportunity:
to pray for someone who is ill,
to write to someone who is lonely,
to show concern for someone who suffers,
to speak lovingly with someone
who is afraid or angry.
Help me today to be less concerned
about my needs and wants,
about things I cannot control or make happen,
and help me touch someone with love.
Then this day will be a great day,
and it will not be wasted in waiting.

TEACH ME HOW TO SOAR

This is your day, O Lord.
You made it; it belongs to you.
And yet you share it with me,
with all of its opportunities and challenges,
its problems and risks.
I thank you for your day, O Lord,
and for whatever it may bring my way.
Keep me from becoming entrapped in its snares,
its corruptions and pitfalls.
Teach me how to soar, my God.
Even while I labor in the valley,
free me to float above the cloud-shrouded,
snow-capped peaks that hover over its edges.
And let me be free to set others free,
to introduce some brother or sister
to that glorious release, that soaring
that is possible for those who are reconciled to you.
This is your day, O Lord.
Help me to live it
according to your plan for my life.

FOR
MY WORK

KEEP ME FAITHFUL

I thank you, O Lord,
that you love and accept me as I am,
and not for what I might accomplish today.
Help me to accept myself as you accept me,
to face this day's problems and challenges
as your child and servant.
It is not so important that I be successful,
but that I be faithful,
that I belong to you,
that I represent and glorify you.
It is important, O God,
that I allow you to have your way
in and through me.
So be it, Lord.

MY ARENA
OF SERVICE

I am grateful, my loving God,
for my arena of service,
for a place to put my feet,
for burdens to carry and lives to touch
in the course of my daily labors.
May I be sensitive to your leading
and to the hurts and needs of people around me.
I step into this day as your messenger and servant.
Help me to be bold, yet full of understanding,
steeped in conviction, yet humble and tolerant
of the convictions of others,
willing to proclaim, yet just as willing to listen,
and ready always to reach out
to someone who is lost and lonely.
And while I am a servant, may I be a student as well,
willing to learn and to grow
in my understanding of life
and your purposes in the world about me.

23

BE PRESENT, LORD

O God, I don't find much contentment in my job.
It is so difficult to believe
that this is your will for my life.
Grant me the courage and strength
to do difficult things today,
and to do them well.
I am going to face things
that I can't handle by myself.
I know you have promised to be present.
Help me to feel your presence
in the difficult hours of this day.

THE NEED
TO PROVE MYSELF

Make me sensitive to your will, O God,
that I may ever be alert
to opportunities to witness
in loving deed and with enlightening word
concerning your gifts of grace and love.
Deliver me from the need to prove myself,
that I may focus on the privilege of manifesting you.
Keep me from manipulating and exploiting people
to gain credits for myself.
Set me free, O Lord, to openly, honestly,
and lovingly represent and reflect you
in my daily relationships.

DULL AND LONELY HOURS

I pray, my Lord,
that you will fill my hours
with a deep sense of your loving presence.
My job is lonely,
devoid of the excitement
of new faces and experiences.
The hours are long and tedious,
and sometimes the drudgery is intolerable.
Yet I am your child,
and I am in this place to carry on your purposes.
I dedicate even the dull and lonely hours
of my life to you, O Lord.
May they serve to accomplish your objectives
in me and through me.

I WANT TO BE APPRECIATED

I'm fed up, O God.
I can't take it any longer—
the scorn, the indifference of my coworkers,
the snickers of those who take advantage of me.
I want something for myself, O Lord—
to walk on water, to heal the sick,
or at least to receive a little appreciation,
to get a medal or a certificate of merit,
or even a commendatory slap on the back.
Give me some measure of success, O God,
some sense of importance,
some mountain on which to be transfigured,
some out-of-this-world experience
to give wings to my flagging spirit.
Forgive me, O God,
for these unworthy and unwarranted feelings.
May the crucible of this life purge me
of my lust for self-esteem
and render me effective as your servant.

STAY WITH ME, LORD

I pray, O Lord,
that being your servant
may always be my primary vocation.
Help me to find some measure of joy
in my labors today,
and to manifest joy
in my personal relationships.
Above all, enable me to be faithful to you,
whatever the circumstances that close in about me.
I am yours, dear Lord;
never leave my side.
Stay with me, Lord;
stay with me.

IN
DIFFICULT
TIMES

WHEN I AM FRIGHTENED

O God, I know all the words designed
to comfort and assure.
I am aware of your promise to stay close beside me,
whatever the crisis that confronts me.
But I am frightened, Lord,
and I cannot evade my anxieties.
Forgive me for my small faith and large doubts,
O Lord,
for finding it so difficult to trust you
on the threshold of this fearful chapter in my life.
You have promised sufficient grace for special trials.
I lay claim to that grace.
I pray that you will help me in some special way
to sense your loving presence
undergirding and overseeing my life
in this time of testing.

WHEN I FACE
A TERRIBLE LOSS

I have suffered a terrible loss, O God,
and I want to believe that you really care—
but you let it happen, Lord,
and I keep asking *why?*
The skies remain cold and gray with merciless silence.
I know I must accept this loss
and learn to live with it;
but the vacuum, the agony, the bitterness and pain
flatten me with despair.
O God, fill the vacuum,
end the agony,
resolve the bitterness,
help me endure the pain,
and let me feel your loving presence
so that I may be grateful for what you have given me,
even if it cannot remain mine forever.
Turn the ashes of my loss
into something beautiful and useful.
I can't do this, dear Lord, but you can.
Do it now, Lord; please do it now.

WHEN I AM DISABLED

I have been incapacitated, my Lord,
and I am facing a long period of resting and waiting.
My normal responsibilities must be shelved,
or placed in the hands of others.
I can no longer do what I was trained to do,
or care for those for whom I am responsible.
I do not see how my life can be of any use now,
to you or to other people.
I pray, O God,
that you will care for those I cannot serve,
that you will fill in the empty spaces
caused by my absence.
Resolve my anxieties
and grant that I may rest in your care.
You have not given me up, O Lord.
Work out your purposes within me,
and enable me to find some way
of serving you and others right here where I am.

WHEN I MUST MAKE A DECISION

I am faced with an important decision, Lord,
and I am concerned that I find your will.
What is the direction you would have me go?
You know my strengths and weaknesses, Lord,
and you know how and where I can best serve you.
You also know my needs, Lord,
and how foolishly I interpret them
and attempt to fulfill them in self-serving ways.
Break through my selfish desires
and my endeavors to build up my ego.
Set me free from self-serving tendencies,
that I may see and fulfill your will and purposes.
Help me, Lord, to make my decision,
not in terms of what it will do for me
or how much I may benefit by it,
but in terms of where I can most effectively
serve you and others about me.

WHEN SOMEONE HURTS ME

Someone stepped on me today, O Lord,
and I reacted in frustration and anger.
I guess I'm pretty fragile; I break so easily.
I am so dependent on
the good wishes and commendations of others.
I did not act like your servant,
but more like a spoiled child still grappling
for some sense of personhood or identity.
I have so much to learn, Lord,
especially about what it means to be
your child, your disciple,
assigned to relate and reflect you
to the people about me.
Set me free, God,
from the need to be the king of some hill,
even the need to be appreciated and respected,
and help me to find my joy and my measure of worth
in your love
and in my relationship to you.

WHEN DEATH DRAWS NEAR

They say that my illness may be terminal,
that there is nothing more medicine can do for me.
I suspected it for some time, O Lord,
and you have already been at work in my life,
with special injections of grace.
Somehow, I am not afraid anymore.
I feel you are near; I sense your loving concern.
All life is terminal on this earth,
but I believe that its end is only the beginning,
another step in your creative process.
I am grateful, Lord, that you are beside me,
that you will accompany me on this new adventure
into regions and experiences
that are beyond human knowledge or comprehension.
Now, my God, I pray for my dear family and friends,
who may not feel your nearness
as clearly as I do in this moment.
Grant them, also, your grace.
Their pain is far greater than mine.
Have your own way, Lord, with me and with them,
for we are yours forever.

WHEN I LOSE MY MATE

She was so precious to me, O Lord,
and now you have taken her from me.
Oh how I loved her, Lord, and needed her!
Next to you, I loved her more than anyone
or anything I have ever known.
There were times when
she was more important to me
than you and your purposes for my life.
And there were far more occasions
when I placed my selfish concerns
far ahead of my love and concern for her.
I pray that you will cover my guilt, O Lord.
You gave her to me, my God,
without the guarantee that I could have her forever.
I am grateful, Lord—
even while my heart cries out in bitterness.
Forgive me that I cannot joyfully
commit her into your hands.
Nevertheless, I commit her to you—reluctantly—
and I pray that your miracle-working grace
will put me together again,
that you will fill the empty places in my life
and renew, encourage, and strengthen me.
She has left me, Lord, but you haven't.
Put my feet in motion again, O Lord,
that I may continue to walk in your paths
and carry on your purposes.

WHEN I FACE SURGERY

My doctor has ordered me into surgery, O God.
It will be one of the rare times in my life
when I relinquish all rights, all control,
the very beat of my heart
into the hands of other human beings.
I am courting some apprehensions, my Lord.
I may manage to hide them from my loved ones,
but you know my fears
as I prepare to gamble with uncertainty
in the valley of shadows.
I don't have to be afraid.
You have promised to stay by my side.
I lay claim to your forgiving and sustaining grace.
I commit my loved ones—
and my own body and being—
into your loving care.
Whether I awaken to carry on
your purposes in this world
or enter into the eternal glory
of your ultimate destiny for me,
this is in your hands, dear Lord;
I am content to leave it there,
to pray that your will be done.

WHEN IT'S DIFFICULT TO LOVE

I have discovered, O Lord, that,
despite my enthusiastic affirmations
and proclamations of your love for humankind,
there are some people I do not like very much.
I have no problem with those
who affirm and support me.
But when it comes to people who attempt to use me,
or have no use for me,
or even have the audacity
to question my motives or criticize my actions,
I feel very little love or concern for them.
While you love and accept me as I am,
even when I fail you or cease to serve you,
I am not capable of loving and accepting those
who do not in some measure serve me.
Inasmuch as I fail to love, I fail to serve you.
I am still basically selfish,
concerned primarily about my own
station and status in life.
Is it possible, Lord, that I have been using you
to fulfill my aspirations
rather than to discover wholeness and fulfillment
in submitting myself to your loving control?
Forgive me, O God, and teach me anew
the meaning of your great love,
and how to love and accept others
as you love and accept me.

WHEN I LOSE MY JOB

I claim to believe your promises, O God,
and I realize I must depend on you.
But now I am frightened by the prospect
of not being able to pay my bills.
I have often taken for granted
the good things that came my way—
even to the point of neglecting you
and failing to walk in your path.
Now, God, I am driven back to you again.
I am desperate for some tangible support,
some evidence of your concern for me
and for those who look to me for material security.
Restore, O God, my confidence in you.
Help me believe that you will continue
to fulfill your promises to care for me,
that you will stay close to me
in these anxious moments.
I have prayed that your will be done;
now help me to believe
that you will answer that prayer,
that you will work out your will in my life,
that this apparent loss may be a step toward
something even more productive
in the months and years before me.
I am yours, O God, and you will never let me go.
Have it your way, Lord,
and grant me the faith to believe
that your way is best.

WHEN A PARENT DIES

We knew it had to happen eventually, Lord,
but it hurts so much when someone so important to us
is suddenly taken away.
And our sorrow is mixed with regret, Lord.
In our pursuit of our own goals
and in fulfilling each other's needs,
we have sometimes neglected our parents—
those who made it possible
for all good things to happen to us.
We thank you for our parents,
who have contributed so much to our lives.
Even while we feel sorrow at their absence,
we would not wish that they be held back
from the beauty and glory you have in store for them.
O Lord, use this experience to deepen
our commitment to your will for our lives,
and lead us into fearless confrontation with death
when we pass from this world
into your eternal domain.
We commend our loved one to your tender care,
O Lord.
She is yours forever.

WHEN I AM DISCOURAGED

I've had it, Lord.
I've honestly tried to serve you,
to love my neighbor,
to share myself and my possessions with others.
But it seems that wherever I go
I run into stone walls.
The very people I reach out to help
turn against me.
I've been conned, derided, abused,
and I just can't take it any longer.
Is it really true, Lord,
that I am expected to be like Christ?
I know the answer, Lord.
It is this to which you have called me.
It is for this that you have
redeemed and commissioned me.
It is because of this hard road
along which you lead me
that you grant me strength to endure,
joy in the midst of suffering,
and the assurance of ultimate victory.
Pull me out of this pit, O Lord.
I don't belong here; I am your child and servant.
Teach me, O God, how to accept my status
and the validity and power that go with it,
and to walk and serve in joy.

OUR
MARRIAGE

THE JOURNEY BEFORE US

We are at the beginning of a new
and wonderful journey, Lord.
We know where we have been—
the sorrows and the joys,
the triumphs and defeats of our past lives.
We do not know what lies ahead.
There will be pitfalls as well as pleasures.
Our hours of happiness will be interrupted
by times of despair.
Mountains will be interspersed with valleys.
The road will sometimes be rough and rutted.
We are grateful, O God,
that we can travel together.
We pray that we may continue
to walk side by side,
supporting each other
and garnering from you and from each other
the grace and strength we need,
discovering in the midst of difficult hours
that deep inner peace and joy of knowing
that we are surrounded by your loving concern
and we need never lose our way.
We enlist our lives in your purposes, Lord.
You are our shepherd, our captain, our companion.
Grant, O God, that we may follow you forever.

LOVE IS NOT EXCLUSIVE

We know, O Lord, that within the human family
our relationship with each other must be primary.
We are to share, even as one,
your gifts, your life, and your purposes,
as well as our sorrows and joys.
But forbid, O God,
that our relationship be exclusive,
that we crowd out or neglect others who love us
and who need to be loved by us.
Enlarge our capacity to love, O Lord.
While we meet so many of each other's needs,
some of our needs must be met by others.
And there are those to whom each of us may transmit
joy and strength and healing
through our caring and loving.
We pray that our love for each other
may stretch our souls
and give us a greater capacity to love others.

WHEN AT ODDS
WITH MY MATE

I am at odds with my mate, O God,
and I can't believe it's all my fault.
Yet I know I have been guilty of trying
to impose my will and even my convictions on her.
I take her for granted and treat her at times
as if she belonged to me.
She belongs to you, O Lord.
You graciously share her with me,
but you forbid that I possess her for myself
or attempt to make her conform to my image.
As you set me free to be myself,
enable me to support and encourage
that gift of freedom for her.
Teach me how to truly love her,
to be close to her in her need—
and yet not so close
as to stifle her in her growth—
to allow her to be what you want her to be,
that she may be whole and happy
and may enrich the lives of others
even as she enriches and blesses my life.

LEARNING HOW TO FORGIVE

Our loving Lord,
you have restored us to you
through the experience of forgiveness;
now teach us how to forgive each other.
We proclaim to each other our love,
but such proclamations are hollow and empty
unless we learn how to forgive.
We claim your forgiving love,
yet we are intolerant
of each other's faults and failings.
We have caused each other much pain.
Rather than forgiving, making up, and starting over,
we crawl into our corners of self-pity
and mope about like foolish, spoiled children.
We know, O Lord, there is no love in such antics—
only pride, hurt feelings, and bruised egos.
May our love for each other
resemble your love for each of us.
Help us to say, "I'm sorry,"
and to embrace each other in forgiving love.

THE JOY OF RECONCILIATION

Thank you, Lord, for the joy of forgiving
and being forgiven.
Something came between us today.
We felt stymied
because we couldn't have our own way.
There were hurt feelings and angry words,
and for hours we felt estranged and lonely.
It seems as if everything comes to an end
when our love is smothered by some silly grievance.
There were moments when we felt
hate toward each other.
Perhaps we were really angry with ourselves,
and we projected our feelings
of inferiority and low worth.
As you love us,
even when we foolishly rebel against you,
as you reach out to forgive and restore us to you,
so teach us that love is stronger than hate
and enable us always to be reconciled to each other.
There is so much happiness in restoring our love.
We thank you for the joy of reconciliation.

RECOGNIZING PRIORITIES

We need to be reminded from time to time, Lord,
that other things in your universe are more important
than our happiness or well-being.
The world is not designed to satisfy
all our sensual or spiritual appetites.
It seems so natural at times to make each other
the focal point of our lives,
and then wonder why we are still
discontented and unfulfilled.
You have graciously allowed us to share our lives,
but our happiness together
is never to be an end in itself.
It is a means of beautifying and enriching our lives
in order to make us more fruitful and effective
in our relationships with others.
As our love for each other grows deeper,
make our commitment to you and to other people
more genuine and demonstrative.
We pray that you and your objectives
may always have priority in our lives.

LISTENING TO EACH OTHER

As we must listen to you
if we are to hear you speak through your Word
and through your children about us,
so we must learn how to listen to each other.
Teach us the art of communication.
Grant each of us the discipline
to turn off self-centered speaking
and seek to hear what the other has to say.
Help us respect the importance
of each other's thoughts and feelings.
Make us sensitive to each other,
that we may learn to recognize
conflicts and needs,
hurts and fears,
delights and joys.
Help us to feel, and to listen, O God,
with loving hearts and attentive minds,
to our beloved mates.

THE JOY OF SERVING

The greatest joy of our lives, O Lord,
is the joy of knowing that we are your children,
that you have appointed and commissioned us
to carry on your objectives in the world about us.
Thank you, our God, for the joy of serving,
for the joy of knowing that,
even when we differ and disagree,
we can discover unity in your love for us
and in sharing your love
with each other and with those around us.
And thank you for the grace,
the gifts and talents that enable us to serve others.
Our roles as individuals may not be the same,
but our goal is one: to advance your kingdom,
to communicate your healing touch of love
to those who suffer
and to those who are lonely or lost.
Let our joy show through, O Lord,
and transmit joy to the dull lives
of unhappy people in our paths.

WHEN WE'RE BORED WITH EACH OTHER

Lord, it seems that the flame needs to be rekindled.
The sparkle has gone out of our relationship—
or at least the fire is burning very low.
O God, we need your special touch on our lives.
Maybe it's the glamor that we miss,
the excitement we once felt
when we held each other close.
Maybe we've been childishly dependent
on ecstatic feelings to shore up our relationship,
and now, when they cool down,
we assume love is lost.
We begin to feel bored with each other.
Perhaps we expect too much.
Help us to concentrate on what we share,
what we are and have together.
Help us to be less concerned about our personal needs
and more committed to serving you
through our service to others.
Lead us, together, to seek our joy from you,
the giver of true and eternal joy,
by concentrating on your objectives for our lives.
Turn up the fire within us, dear God,
that our lives and our relationship may glow again
and the lives of others may be warmed
and blessed through us.

WHEN WE
HURT EACH OTHER

We are fragile, Lord;
we break so easily.
We often act like spoiled children
still reaching for personhood or identity.
We both insist on our own way—
and we expect the other to subscribe
to our own imperfections.
We react in frustration and anger
when one or the other is not always
generous and kind and understanding.
Thus we hurt each other,
and the day is wasted
in pouting and self-pity.
Forgive us, Lord, and teach us
how to forgive each other quickly.
Heal these foolish hurts we cause each other.
Rid us of the selfish distortions
threatening our relationship.
Restore us to your loving heart,
and immerse us in your total and perfect love.

HELP US PRAY TOGETHER

We are wondering, our Lord,
why it seems so awkward, at times, to pray together.
Do we still regard our individual relationships to you
as something personal and private?
Or are we drifting away from each other,
assuming that our prayer lives have little in common?
We love you, and we love each other,
and yet it is often difficult to express ourselves
openly and honestly in the other's presence.
Grant that each of us will allow the other
the right to maintain
an individual prayer relationship with you,
even the right to hold back from the other
thoughts and feelings that we share only with you.
We know praying together
can be joyous and enriching,
that it continues to bind us to you and to each other.
Teach us, our great God,
how to sing and pray and praise you
together.

OUR REASON FOR LIVING

Teach us, our loving God,
how to put first things first,
how to make your objectives
most important in our lives.
We are so very important to each other.
Our children's welfare
is more dear to us than life itself.
Most of our hours of each day
go to feeding and clothing ourselves and our family.
And yet achieving physical well-being is not
our central vocation, our reason for living.
You are our Lord and our Master.
Everything else about us is subservient
to your will and design for our lives.
Help us, O Lord,
to keep our loyalties and allegiances
in the proper order
and to discover that true joy is found only
in a faithful and obedient relationship to you.

TEACH US
TO LAUGH

Surely you must be amused
at the foolish things we do, O Lord.
Teach us how to laugh at ourselves,
at the petty things that come between us.
There would be less anger and agony
if there were more laughter,
if we took some things less seriously,
if we learned how to tolerate the slip of the tongue
or the slight misunderstanding,
even the little faults and failings,
the oddities and idiosyncrasies of each other.
Make our laughter the laughter of love,
that becomes a hymn of thanksgiving and praise
to you who have made our love ever more real
and our relationship ever more meaningful.

OUR FAMILY

A BABY
ON THE WAY

A baby is on the way, Lord,
and our hearts are filled with ever-increasing delight
as we marvel at the awesome mystery
of being cocreators with you.
We are grateful for this blessed privilege.
Even while we parents-to-be rejoice
in being the recipients of your love
and the instruments of your will,
we regard with apprehension
this responsibility that is ours.
We feel so much
the need of relating more deeply to you.
As we cling more closely to each other,
we commit ourselves to you,
resting in the confidence
that this baby is in your embrace,
that you will care for our child and for us.
We pray that each of us and our child may be
your children and your beloved servants forever.

WHEN A CHILD IS BORN

You have presented to us a lovely child, O God,
and our hearts are almost exploding with gratitude.
You have blessed us with a wonder-filled token
of your love for us
and of your trust in us as your servants.
Grant us, loving Lord,
the grace to believe that with this gift
are also given the strength and wisdom
to faithfully carry out our responsibility.
This delightful creature is your child, O God.
We are privileged to enjoy her
and commissioned to share our lives with her.
Accept our thanksgiving
for this beautiful gift, our Lord.
We willingly receive the joys and the sorrows,
the comfort and the pain,
that accompany the gift of this child.
We dedicate ourselves
to bringing her up as your child,
and we pray that she may love and serve you always.

PRESENTATION OF A CHILD

It is with pride and with joy
that we bring our child to you, our Lord.
We honor and praise you, O God,
as we dedicate this precious life to you.
We know that he belongs to you,
that your Spirit abides within him,
that we, child and parents,
are really brothers and sisters
within the family of God.
How grateful we are for your confidence in us,
for the privilege and responsibility
of shepherding him through the years
of childhood and youth!
We claim your grace and your wisdom
for this awesome task.
Help us to be faithful in our assignment.
And bless and keep our young one,
that he may someday hear your call to service
and take up his cross to follow you.

ENTRUSTING OUR CHILDREN TO GOD

O God, the task of rearing our children
is a frightening responsibility.
It is with fear and trembling
that we accept this awesome charge,
trusting that with the responsibility
is also granted the grace we so much need
to meet this challenge successfully.
It is a task beyond our abilities,
and we need your special help to do
the job we have been commissioned to do.
It is also a blessed calling,
and we are amazed and gratified that you
chose to entrust us with it.
We know we are neither worthy nor qualified,
but we believe that you will be with us and help us,
and somehow through us work out
your purposes with our young ones.
As we will be enriched through these children,
so grant that they may be made rich in love and joy
by way of your Spirit through us.
We entrust them to you, dear Lord.
We know that, even when they turn from you,
you will never give them up.
Pursue them, O God; stay close to them.
We pray that whatever paths they travel
will ultimately lead them back to you
and to the light of your purposes for their lives.

AFRAID FOR OUR CHILDREN

We are fearful for our children, dear Lord.
They are continuously exposed
to the hazards of this life
and the atrocities of our world.
They are constantly under the influence of people
who do not share our beliefs
for life's goals and objectives.
The values we have tried to pass on to them
are perpetually challenged by the society
in which they live and move.
O God, we can't shield them from the world
and its influences
or from life and its realities.
We continue to commit these dear ones to you.
We pray that, while we cannot
impose our values on them,
we can discover true life and purpose
in a relationship of love and trust in you,
and demonstrate by our living
the joy of being your servants and disciples.
Grant, O God, that we may reflect you
rather than promote or program you
in the lives of our children.
Bless them, Lord, that they may belong to you forever.

THANKS FOR OUR CHILDREN

We have always been grateful, O Lord,
for our children,
the precious ones you have committed to our care.
We have, however, been fearful and anxious at times,
and sometimes irresponsible as their parents.
We have sought to possess them
and have used them to fill the emptiness of our lives
and sometimes to camouflage our failures.
We have found our joy in them
and exercised our hostilities on them.
Yet in our selfish way
we loved them and sacrificed for them,
wanting desperately that they be happy and successful
in the course of their lives.
We have failed at times
to recognize our stewardship, O Lord,
and have attempted to mold them in accordance
with our short-sighted and limited aspirations.
And we have often failed in our most important task
with these dear ones:
to demonstrate a loving commitment to you
and to the human family throughout the world.
Help us to live in such a way, dear Lord,
that our children will know that we have discovered
that real life and eternal joy
and ultimate worth and meaning come by way
of a loving and trusting relationship with you.

WHEN A CHILD IS ILL

Somehow, our loving God,
all of our disagreements and differences
seem to disappear as we pray together
for the healing of our beloved child.
We fear submitting to your will
if it means the loss of this one who is so dear to us.
We honestly do not see how we could find
any joy or purpose in life
apart from our child's continued love and laughter.
And yet this little one is as important to you
as he is to us.
Truly, he is your child—your gift to us—
and we can entrust him to you
and believe that your will shall come to pass.
This we do, O Lord,
and while we pray and hope for his healing,
we pray for the grace to accept your loving will,
which is always good and right,
even when it is beyond our understanding.

LISTENING TO OUR CHILDREN

It is so easy, O Lord,
to tell our children what they ought to be
or what they ought to do.
We often forget that they are real people,
with real feelings and fears, desires and ambitions.
Rather than seek to understand them,
we attempt to program them,
insisting that they conform to our image,
trying to mold them into replicas of ourselves.
They are at times so lovely,
at times so cantankerous,
but they are your children, Lord,
filled with your Spirit.
We want so much for them to develop and mature
in accordance with your will and plan for their lives.
Teach us to treat them as persons,
even while we must lovingly discipline them.
Teach us to listen to them—
their childish explosions of anger and frustration,
their doubts, fears, joys, and pains—
even to share with them our joys and frustrations,
so they may know we are all your fallible children.
Help us to truly love them,
and grant that they may feel assured of that love.

WHEN OUR CHILDREN REBEL

We are worried about our children, Lord.
They are rebelling.
They seem at times to be indifferent
to you and your purposes.
We can't help but feel that we are to blame
when they take off on their precarious journeys,
flirting with those demons of darkness
that are capable of destroying their souls.
We know, O God, that our love for them
cannot coerce them into goodness,
any more than your divine and eternal love
can compel us to follow you.
Maybe we are too absorbed in our own failures
and embarrassed by our inability to lead them aright.
Perhaps our love is selfish—
we don't love them enough to let them go,
even if we can't hold them back.
Help us, O God, to love them as you love us,
patiently and perpetually,
whatever their decisions and actions.
And, though we cannot program their lives
to fit into our agenda for them,
help us to live in a way
that will lovingly influence them
and eventually draw them back to you.
We claim your forgiveness for our failures, O Lord,
and place these dear ones in your loving care.

WHEN OUR CHILD DIES

You gave us the most beautiful gift
we have ever known, O God,
and then you took it away.
There are moments
when we wish we had never known
the joy of this amazing gift,
this lovely child you entrusted to our care.
Maybe we were not worthy, God,
or faithful stewards of this charge
that you placed in our hands.
In moments of bitterness, God,
we are tempted to accuse you of cruelty,
and we dare to doubt your concern and your love.
Yet we believe you are a gentle Father
who forgives our yesterdays
and blesses our tomorrows
and who knows the pain we endure today.
We can only pray that you will enable us to feel
what we know we ought to express—
gratitude for the time your gift was entrusted to us,
for the supreme happiness that was ours together.
You have taken our child, O Lord.
Only you know the reason.
We thank you because we know she is yours forever.

WHEN OUR DAUGHTER MARRIES ❧

She is your wonderful gift to us, O Lord,
this lovely daughter of ours,
our pride, our joy, our precious possession.
She illuminated our dark nights
and brightened our difficult days.
She helped make our marriage
meaningful and worthwhile.
Even when we were at odds with each other,
we were united in our love for her.
We know our love is often selfish,
for there is pain intermixed with joy
as we think of her leaving our family
to share her life with another.
Yet we are more concerned about her happiness
than about our feelings of loneliness,
and we pray for your blessing
upon her marriage with the man she loves.
Grant them much joy, O God.
Watch over them and keep them,
and may the fruits of their marriage
bring as much happiness to them
as our children have brought to us.

WHEN THE FAMILY IS TOGETHER

Whether it be a picnic at the park
or an evening meal at home,
the gathering of the family should be
a time of celebration,
a religious experience,
with or without sermons or scripture lessons.
We pray that it might be so with us, our Lord,
that we might find joy as we come together,
that we will bypass any bickering,
overcome our misunderstandings,
and know the inner contentment
of family love and unity.
We all belong to you, O God,
and are members of your divine family.
As we relate to you,
may we relate in love to one another,
that we may gather often as a family
to sing songs of love
and shout praises to you,
our Lord and our God.

THANK YOU
FOR OUR HOME

It means much to us, dear Lord,
to have a place to live, a place to call our own.
It is a place for our love to grow and blossom
like the flowers and trees surrounding our home.
It is a place for us to share with others
who may find shelter under its roof
and warmth within its rooms.
It is a sanctuary from the rush of the marketplace
and the noise of busy streets,
a place to live and love and laugh and cry.
It may not be ours for long, O God,
but while you have placed this home
under our stewardship,
we gratefully dedicate it to you and your purposes
and celebrate the privilege of living together
within its walls.
Forbid, O God, that it become a prison
that confines us to selfish living,
or an anchor that prevents us from pursuing
your objectives throughout our world.
Make it always a place of prayer,
of rest and renewal,
of preparation for consecrated service
to you and your children.

WHEN FINANCES FRUSTRATE

We become frustrated and fearful, O God,
when we can't make ends meet,
when our outgo threatens to surpass our income.
We have already learned
that we can't have everything we want.
Now it appears we may have to forego
some things we always assumed we needed.
Even while we must prepare for the future,
teach us how to live one day at a time,
to seek first your kingdom,
and to worry less about what may happen tomorrow.
You have promised to care for us, O God.
Help us to trust in your promises and to discover,
even in the disagreeable circumstances
that threaten us,
the importance of walking with you
and dedicating our lives to your objectives.
Show us, our Lord,
how to be good stewards of those gifts
you have placed in our hands.
Teach us that, regardless of financial difficulties
that come our way,
we can find our joy in you.

CELEBRATING OUR VACATION

We are grateful, our loving God,
that we can celebrate together
this place of beauty
and this time of rest and relaxation.
We know you were present with us
in the tensions of the city
and the demands of each working day.
And there is beauty to be found
in busy streets and shopping centers,
the offices and institutions
that seek to supply the needs and wants
of this world's multitudes.
Yet no other beauty matches
the breathtaking grandeur of this place, O Lord.
We would like to build a shrine here, Lord,
but it would only mar
the majestic works of your hands.
Thus we raise our voices in celebration
and pray that our refreshed spirits will glow
with the love and joy and beauty
we have found together in this place.
Help us to share our blessings
when we return to the city
by bringing joy
to our tired and unhappy sisters and brothers.

BREAKING OLD TIES

We are about to move away, Lord,
to pull up deeply embedded roots,
to leave behind this friendly environment
and seek out a new place in which to live and work.
We're excited as we anticipate the adventures
of new places and new faces,
but we also feel the pain
of leaving behind the familiar,
of confining to memory alone
the beautiful experiences and relationships
we have known here.
Overcome our apprehensions, dear Lord,
and enable us to meet the challenge before us.
While we express our gratitude
for the friends and the great times we have had here,
help us to assume a place of responsibility
in a new community and among a new people.
May we never forget, O Lord,
that we are sent by you,
that we are your servants forever,
that you go before us and will always be with us.
We pray that you will prepare our hearts
for this new arena of service to you
and to our new neighbors for your sake.

WORSHIPING TOGETHER

How delightful it is, our great God,
to gather together the frayed ends
of our lives and our relationships
and focus our attention and concern
on your love and grace,
to declare your worth and celebrate your presence.
Whether we worship in private or in public,
our worship clears the air
and brings peace back to the soul
and assures us once more that your power
is always available to help us
over the rough spots in the road.
It is in the hour of worship
that we are renewed in our relationships
to you and to one another
and rededicated to your course for our lives.
Truly you are a great God
and we are your beloved children.
We sing to your glory, our God,
and shout your praises!

FOR
SPECIAL
PEOPLE

THANK YOU FOR PEOPLE

Thank you for people, Lord—
short and tall, fat and small,
money-grabbers, pleasure-seekers, attention-getters,
the bold and the fearful,
the commanders and the demanders.
Some weep and whine; others curse and carouse.
Some are benign and some are belligerent.
Whoever they are, they are your creatures,
and you love them as you love me.
It is your will that I love them as well,
and serve you through serving them.
It is so often through these very people,
whatever their exterior appearance,
that I see you reflected and hear you speak.
Rid me of self-concern, O Lord,
that I may be free and open
to your manifestations through others,
and that they may see you
reflected in my attitudes and actions.

THANK YOU
FOR MY FRIEND

I thank you for my friend, dear Lord.
You reached out through his devotion and concern
to kindle a new fire within me.
He broke through my apathy and depression
to reveal the beauty and fragrance of life about me.
He marched into my jungle of despair,
sliced through my confusion,
and gave order and motivation
to my purposeless gropings.
I am grateful, O God, to you and for him.
I pray that you will use me,
as you have so graciously used him,
to transmit joy to your joyless, despairing children
who cross my path.
And bless my friend, O God;
keep him and use him forever.

A FRIEND
IN TROUBLE

I pray, O Lord,
for my friend who is in serious trouble.
He's blinded by the excitement of the moment, Lord,
and doesn't realize how much his actions are
hurting himself and his loved ones.
He is a good man.
Bringing hurt or harm to someone else is
the last thing he would ever want.
Deal gently with him, Lord,
but stop him before he goes too far.
Bring him back to your will,
to the joy and purposefulness
that once marked the actions
of this one who is my friend.

THE MARRIAGE OF FRIENDS

Our great and loving God,
whose eternal love has now united
our dear friends in the relationship of marriage,
grant them now and forever
the grace to live in accordance with your Word
and to follow together in your footsteps.
Sustain them in their faith and affection
toward each other;
watch over them and stay close to them
in all the trials and conflicts of this life.
Send them forth as your servants
to exemplify and demonstrate toward each other,
and in their relationships to other people,
your great love for all humanity.
We commit them to your care, O God,
and pray that you will keep them forever.

FOR A FRIEND
WHO IS ILL

I am praying for my friend who is so very ill.
O my Lord, you brought the touch of healing
to those who crossed your path in your earthly life.
You promised to respond to the prayers
of your children who struggle to follow
and reflect you on this earth.
Reach out now to this one with your healing touch.
She belongs to you, O God.
She yearns so deeply to serve you.
Restore her to life and wholeness once more.
And even while she suffers,
may she sense your nearness
and be embraced by your peace.
Grant that she may have joy
even in the midst of her suffering.
And grant, blessed Lord,
that she might get well again.

WHEN I'VE HURT SOMEONE

O my God, I've hurt someone deeply,
someone who trusted in me,
who thought I was strong and loyal and true.
In causing him pain, I have caused you great pain.
I am so human, so frail, and so very foolish.
And I am sorry, Lord.
I would rather have died than let this happen.
But it has happened,
and I can only turn to you for forgiveness
and for restoration to you and your purposes.
I plead with you, my God, to heal his hurt.
My love, if it be love at all,
is selfish and distorted.
Your love is perfect and total and eternal.
Hold him close, O God,
and draw me back into your loving heart,
helping me to love the way you love.

FOR SOMEONE WHO IS DEPRESSED

I am praying, O Lord,
for someone who has a big problem.
She is your child and disciple,
the object of your love and concern,
and she is important to those around her.
She has been laid low with discouragement
and flattened by depression.
She feels that you are looking the other way,
too busy with other things
to pay much attention to her.
So she withdraws into herself
and grieves in her despair.
You know her misery;
you know how much she needs you.
You are the answer to her deepest longings.
Draw her to you, O God.
Enable her to feel your touch of healing
on her crippled spirit.
Even in this moment,
help her to feel that you are near to her
and to see some flicker of light on her dark path.
Grant her your grace, O Lord,
for she belongs to you.

THANKS FOR MY FAMILY

I thank you, O God, for my family.
I pray that I may be faithful and responsible to them,
even as I seek to be faithful to you.
Forbid, O God,
that my love be confined to them alone,
or that I selfishly possess or exploit them
for my own needs.
You and your purposes are primary.
There are others I must love and serve
in the world about me.
Yet I must pray, O God,
that I do not neglect these who are dearest to me.
May our love for one another stretch our souls
and enlarge our capabilities to love other people.
And may we all abide in your love forever.

FOR OUR PASTOR

We pray for our pastor, dear Lord.
We can only guess about the pressures besieging him,
but we ought to be aware of his humanity,
his weaknesses and his strengths,
his need for human love and concern.
We know how easy it is for us
to expect superhuman feats from this person,
to assume that he has
some special arrangements with you,
some special grace or gift
that will enable him to meet our needs,
calm our fears, eliminate our conflicts,
and make for us a kind of heaven in this world.
You sent him to us in response to our prayers.
But you sent us a man, not a god,
with needs and wants like those of any other man,
and with temptations and conflicts
that may be greater than those of most others.
Help us, our loving God, to love him, respect him,
confide in him, listen to him, be patient with him,
excuse and forgive him.
And help us, his coministers,
to assist him in advancing
your kingdom in our world.

84

FOR OUR CONGREGATION

Bless our church, O God,
and the many who make up our congregation.
We are obstinate and rebellious children,
often oblivious to the needs of one another.
You are patient with us, our loving God,
and you have not given us up.
Teach us how to love one another
and how to act like your loving sons and daughters
rather than jealous children fighting
for recognition and acceptance.
Draw us together in unity and strength,
so the people of our community
may see that you are God
and may sense through us
some measure of your love for them.

FOR AGED PARENTS

We pray, our great God, for our aged parents,
and for the elderly saints about us
who have retired from active service
to wait your call to far better things.
We are here because of the sacrifices and risks
they took on our behalf.
They were faithful servants,
and they communicated your love and grace to us.
We love these dear people,
but we often neglect them
in our persistent grasping
for recognition and security.
We take them for granted,
assuming their needs are met
and their desires fulfilled.
Bless them, O God.
Warm their hearts
with an intense sense of your presence.
And help us, O God,
to see their needs,
to feel something of their loneliness,
and to be channels of your love and grace to them.

FOR LOVED ONES FAR AWAY

My thoughts today are of dear ones who are far away.
How much I love them and long for them!
I want so much to be with them,
to share their laughing or their crying,
to help bear their heavy loads,
to comfort them in their anxieties and illnesses.
O Lord, you know their problems, their hurts,
their joys and their sorrows.
You are with them, near to them,
even as you are with me.
They are your children—
my sisters and brothers in your eternal kingdom—
and you love them with a pure, everlasting love.
I pray that you will heal them where they hurt
and give them strength to overcome their obstacles.
Flood their lives even now
with a renewed sense of your presence,
with the joy of knowing your concern about them,
whatever their circumstances.
Hold them close to your loving heart,
that they may never stray from you
and your course for their lives.
May our mutual faith in you
deepen our love for one another,
even as our service for you now separates us
one from the other.
Bless them and keep them, dear Lord,
these dear ones who are so far away.

MY RELATIONSHIP WITH GOD

I NEED A VISION

My great God, I am still learning how to walk.
I believe that you walk beside me,
even in my mundane, ordinary, everyday living.
I know I can worship you
even as I walk through busy streets,
in the frantic, tension-filled hours of the daily grind.
There are times, however,
when I need to soar—
to see mountaintops and colorful sunsets,
to hear majestic chorales,
to meditate on profound philosophies,
to look beyond the dusty valleys
where people sweat and swear
and struggle and suffer.
I ask not that you remove me from the valley,
or for escape or refuge.
I ask only that my heart and imagination
be enriched and inspired
with visions transcending the commonplace,
and that you grant me the grace
to translate such visions into words and deeds
that will enrich my life and
the lives of earthbound men and women about me.

WHEN I FAIL

I have failed again, O Lord.
Despite my firm resolutions and determined efforts,
I have flopped—fallen on my face.
It is difficult to believe, dear Lord,
that this does not come between me and you,
that you still refuse to give me up,
that your grace is sufficient
in spite of my frailties and faults.
It is thus that I fall, only to rise again,
I am wounded in battle, only to fight on another day.
And it is thus that I come limping back to you.
Forbid, O God, that I should ever be so broken,
so beaten down,
that I fail to come limping back.
Pull me to my feet again, O God.
Grant to me the assurance of ultimate victory,
that I may be strong and faithful.

WHEN THE FIRE BURNS LOW

This is the hour of worship, O God,
and I feel dull and lethargic.
My soul is as gray as fog.
The inner fires have died out.
I hear and I read your words—
but they are just words.
Even the music that used to set my heart singing
is at this moment but weird sounds
going in different directions.
I can't feel grace or respond to challenge.
I know you are somewhere about, my Lord,
that my feelings are no measure of your nearness.
But I need to feel good sometimes, O God.
Forbid that I pin my faith on what I may feel,
but grant some sense of your presence in this hour,
that I may sing your praises
and worship you with joy.
Turn up the fire within me, dear God,
that my life might glow again
and the lives of others may be warmed through me.

CLAIMING GOD'S GRACE

I have sinned against you, God,
and against my friend.
Because of my self-centeredness,
my grappling to meet my needs and satiate my senses,
to nullify my loneliness and boost my ego,
I have hurt someone you love.
I can think of excuses, Lord—
my humanity, my weaknesses,
the circumstances under which I live and work.
You do not, however, accept my excuses;
you only offer me your grace.
Your grace is always available.
I claim it anew, dear God.
Envelop me in your care
and enable me to truly love—
the kind of love that will heal my friend's wounds
and bring to each of us joy and strength once more.

A MEMBER OF GOD'S FAMILY

I thank you, my great God,
for you made it possible for me to know who I am.
You have touched me with your cleansing power
and placed your Spirit in my heart.
I am your child,
even while I am fallible and often very foolish.
I am your servant—and I am to serve you
by serving my brothers and sisters about me.
I am redeemed by your love,
sanctified through your righteousness,
ordained by your calling,
empowered with your grace.
I am destined to represent your purposes
and to demonstrate and communicate your love
to those who cross my path.
Thank you, God, for making me valid and significant,
for putting meaning and purpose into my life,
for snatching me out of the pit of self-centeredness
and restoring my identity
as a member of your eternal family.

FOR FAITHFULNESS

I know, O Lord, that I have always belonged to you.
I know, as well,
that I have often tried to run from you,
foolishly thinking that happiness and adventure
were somewhere out there
with the bright lights and the laughing crowd.
I feel a little lonely, Lord,
because so many of my friends
are not with me in the faith
and do not know you as I do.
But I am thankful you led me
to the decision and the determination
to surrender my life to you and your purposes.
And my heart is filled with joy—
the kind of joy that bright lights and laughing crowds
could never bring.
You are my Savior and my Master.
This is the way I want it—now and always.
I know that I will not always feel close to you,
but I know that you will forever be by my side,
that I never need to be afraid,
because you will never leave me.
Help me, O God, to be faithful to you,
to be your child and your servant
wherever you may lead me
and whatever may be the trials and tribulations
that cross my path.

LOOKING AT THE CROSS

O God, I gaze at the cross
of your Son, Jesus Christ,
and I discover in its terrible pain
the joy and peace of forgiven sin
and the freedom to live in loving relationships
with other people.
I discover, as well,
that I too am destined for pain,
that there are crosses for me to bear
in my journey through life.
It is this to which you have called me.
It is for this
that I have been redeemed and commissioned.
It is because of this hard road
along which you lead me
that you grant me strength to endure,
joy in the midst of suffering,
and the guarantee of final victory.
I thank you, my loving God,
that you who brought the promise of life
to all people through the cross of Christ
will turn the small crosses of my life
into agents of redemption and channels of love
to those I may touch
on my pilgrimage through this world.

YOU ARE HERE, LORD

O God, sometimes I am frightened
by the insecurities about me.
I am sorely tempted to run for my life,
to take refuge in some foolish escapade
that dims the vision or drugs the soul.
But you are my place of refuge, O Lord.
You are here,
and you are aware of my fears and apprehensions.
You can transform my fears into a faith
that will draw me closer to you
and serve to perform your purposes in my life.
I thank you, God, because you are here in my world.
Even among the difficult circumstances
that plague my life,
I know I can find security in you.

SERVANTHOOD
AND
DISCIPLESHIP

I AM YOUR SERVANT

I understand, O God,
that my response to your great love
must be commitment.
You have not only redeemed me
and adopted me as your child;
you have chosen and appointed me
to be your servant.
Your claims upon my life
are what make me significant,
and my living worthwhile.
Yet I have compromised
in responding to your claims,
or ignored them altogether.
Discipleship promises not softness, but suffering,
not comfort, but challenge,
not security, but sacrifice.
I must learn, my Lord,
that my service to you must be rendered
to your human creatures about me.
I offer sacrifices to you
on the altar of other people's needs.
I am to be, in some amazing manner,
a visible member of your divine personhood,
reaching out to help and heal.
O God, you have entrusted me
with great responsibility.
Help me to be your faithful and effective servant.

A WORLD
OF CRISES

I live, my God, within ongoing crisis,
the crisis of revolution
in a churning, conflict-ridden world.
It is frightening.
My reaction at times is
retreat to the sanctuary of the past
where I assume I can be free
from the everyday tensions of this life.
I look to my church
where I hear those great words
about my security and safety in you.
Yet you forbid, O God,
that I run away from this crisis.
You came to "set fire to the earth,"
and revolution is, in part,
a consequence of your Word to us.
You have placed me in the midst of crises, O God.
They are all about me.
Help me, undergirded by your grace,
filled with your Spirit,
to find my place in a revolutionary world,
to put my reputation, job, income, even my life
on the line to confront violence with courage
and hatred with love,
to be your faithful child and servant
in the midst of crises.

AM I DOING ENOUGH?

I feel guilty, Lord.
In a world full of pain—I am blessed.
While millions of my sisters and brothers
are deprived and oppressed,
I am happy and secure.
I am concerned about others, my God,
and I do reach out to those in need,
but I fear that I am not doing enough.
Daily I see vivid revelations of the suffering masses.
More and more, I understand how I contribute
to the poverty and injustice that afflict them.
With your Word constantly challenging me
to assume some sense of responsibility
for the plight of the world's inhabitants,
I discover how shallow
my understanding of discipleship really is.
I need to be converted all over again—
to the kind of discipleship Jesus revealed
and the apostles and early Christians emulated.
I am so far removed from such
servanthood and devotion
that it frightens me.
Have mercy, O God,
and grant that I, by your grace,
will do all you have empowered me to do
in this broken world.

I AM EXPENDABLE

O God, I have assumed I could enjoy
all the benefits of your grace
and still revel irresponsibly
in all the good fortune—
health, talents, possessions—
that have come my way.
I have cheapened your eternal grace
by selfishly grasping your love and promises
for my benefit alone.
Now I am beginning to understand what it means
to belong to you,
to be your possession, your child and servant.
It means that I am expendable.
I am set free from needing
bodily security or comfort—
set free to suffer, even to die, on behalf of others
so I can tell them of your liberating love.
I can't do it; I won't do it—in my own strength.
I have little inclination
to live or to love as you wish—
unless, O Lord, your Spirit can change me
from a sponge greedily sopping up
all I can get from you
into a fruit-bearing branch that exists to serve others.
Work out in me the desire and courage,
my Savior and Master,
to take up my cross and follow you.

EQUIPPED TO SERVE

From you, O God,
I have the credentials for servanthood,
and by your mercy and divine power,
you have equipped me for the task before me.
You have entrusted to your redeemed child
the responsibility of carrying on
the incarnation of Jesus Christ.
You have commissioned me to do
what Christ in his humanity
cannot do in our century.
And you have equipped me for this task
by dwelling in me through your Spirit.
You have, indeed, granted through your Spirit
everything I need to serve you
by serving the people around me.
Help me, as I acknowledge this,
to really believe it—
to act as if this is so whether I feel it or not,
to lay claim to your power,
allowing your Holy Spirit to work
in and through my life.
You have set me free from sin's guilt and power
and eternal consequences
to reconcile me to your divine family;
you have given me your Spirit.
Now send me forth to lovingly and courageously
carry out your purposes
among the people I meet along the way.

PRACTICING WHAT CHRIST PREACHES

Whatever my avocations may be, O God,
my vocation in life is to serve you—
and that means serving your created children
on your behalf.
All my other activities are of lesser importance
and must yield to you and your purposes.
Forgive me, Lord, for my foolish excuses,
for procrastinating when I should be emulating
the proclamations and activities of Jesus Christ.
I feel so helpless when I think of my responsibility
for the uncountable millions of your suffering people,
my very sisters and brothers, throughout the world.
And yet I shirk my responsibility, your charge to me,
even with those I can reach around me.
There are things you will enable me to do:
to consume less, that others may have more;
to use gifts and talents entrusted to me
in enriching the lives of people around me;
to relate to those who suffer,
those who have serious needs I may help fulfill.
Grant me, O Lord, the will and the courage,
not only to listen to your Word
as revealed through Christ,
but to risk all in the blessed endeavor
to put it to work
in my arena of service and responsibility.

THE THINGS
OF THE WORLD

You have been so very good to me, O Lord.
My adversities have been few,
and your gifts have been abundant.
While I am grateful for these tangible gifts,
I have been threatened by the tyranny of things
and have often yielded to the temptation
to possess them for myself.
I lay claim to your forgiving love
and pray for the grace to yield them back to you
and for the wisdom to use things entrusted to my care
for the accomplishment of your purposes
in the world about me.
I am your appointed steward, O Lord.
Lest the things of this world stifle and choke out
my relationship to you,
teach me, in response to your love,
how to make them work for you—
and how to fashion them into ways and means
of enriching the lives of others.

TEACH ME HOW TO LOVE

O God, before I can be a disciple of Jesus Christ
and a servant to other people,
I must learn how to love.
Teach me, Lord, how to love your children,
whatever their race or creed or station in life,
to love them even as you love me
and all your other creatures.
It is my self-centeredness, my self-idolatry,
that prevents your love from flowing through me
to the lonely, unloved, deprived,
and oppressed people in my path.
May your great, eternal love so flood my life that,
not only will my self-serving be forgiven,
but it will be eradicated from my life,
that I may open myself to others
and become a channel
of your gracious and everlasting love to them.
I can't do this through my feeble efforts;
only you can accomplish such a change in my life.
Do it, Lord, whatever the cost or consequence,
for I truly want to be your disciple and servant,
as long as I am permitted to live in this world.

PRAISE
AND
THANKS

PREPARING FOR CHRISTMAS

We could not find you, our loving God,
so you have sought us out.
Prepare our hearts so we may recognize anew
the eternal significance of your coming to us
through your Son, Jesus Christ.
You have come, O Lord, and you continue to come
into the hearts of all those who are open to you
and to your will for their lives.
May your coming give us strength
in our many conflicts
and throw light on the dark paths we must travel
in our disjointed and violent world.
Make us ready for this season of celebration,
that we may receive you and serve you forever,
and make us the vehicles and messengers
of your gifts of grace
to the hearts and lives of others.

GOD HAS COME

Great God, you have come to us.
You have made yourself known
to our world through your Son.
You came by way of the stable and the manger
and the womb of a woman.
And you came to be my Savior and my King.
I have seen the light.
I have heard the Word
that announced the great event,
the glorious happening of your coming to us.
You have broken through
the distortions and darkness of sin
to prepare a way of salvation
for every human creature.
Enable me now, O God,
to follow that One you have sent
and to discover the joys of your love and grace.

GOD IS HERE— LET'S CELEBRATE!

You are here, O God; you are now!
It is time for celebration!
Your promises have been proclaimed
throughout the ages.
With voice and musical instruments,
with lovely melodies and joyful sounds,
your name has been heralded
and your great words celebrated.
Now it is our turn to worship you,
to announce your presence and loving concern
for the inhabitants of this world.
Help us, O God, to fill our homes and sanctuaries,
our halls of learning, our offices of government,
our streets and marketplaces,
with the glad, joyful sounds of celebration.

AN EPIPHANY PRAYER

Eternal God, we cannot see the star
that led the Wise Men to the birthplace of your Son,
but we can know by faith your presence
and power in our lives.
The Jesus who was born in Bethlehem
can be born anew in us
and can live in and through us
who inhabit the world today.
It has happened, O Lord.
You abide within us, and you go before us.
Whatever may befall us on our course
through this fractured world,
may we follow unafraid
and faithfully carry out your purposes.

CHRIST IS ALIVE!

You are alive, O Christ; you are real!
You have overcome death once and for all.
You have demonstrated your great power
in rising from the grave.
How foolish I have been in doubting such power
in the midst of my small problems and many frailties!
Now I know once more
that nothing that may confound or perplex me
is too great for you.
I pray, O God,
that the power that raised Christ from the dead
may raise me out of my fears and failures
to share in that great resurrection
and to celebrate forever
your victory over sin and death.

RESURRECTION POWER

Our loving God,
you who raised Jesus Christ from the dead,
lest this divine miracle be in vain,
show us how the power of the resurrection
can be applied to our personal lives.
Raise us from our graves of defeat and despair
and send us forth to reflect and to demonstrate
your resurrection power to others in our world.
Touch others through us, O God, with that power,
that they may be raised from the dead
to live and serve and praise you forever.

GOD IS WITHIN US

O God, you took your Son from our midst
only to return to us
by way of your invisible Spirit.
Enable us, though we cannot see you
and even when we cannot feel your presence
through some mystical, supernatural experience,
to know that you dwell within us
and are here with us in our fellowship together.
May your Holy Spirit so abide in our hearts
and guide our activities,
that we may walk in your paths
and accomplish those things you would have us do.
Thank you, Lord, for coming to us,
for the gift of your Spirit,
for redeeming us and commissioning us
to be your children and your servants,
your vessels and vehicles,
in extending your kingdom
in this world about us.

PREPARING FOR HOLY COMMUNION

We praise you, our Lord,
for the prophets and apostles
who brought your eternal Word to us,
and for those who proclaim and minister that Word
to our needy spirits.
We praise you, O God, for your Son, our Savior,
the Word made flesh for our salvation.
We give thanks because
you are aware of the human condition
and of our need to more tangibly experience
that Word through Holy Communion.
We have recognized our wrongdoings
and embraced your forgiving and accepting grace.
Now we pray that we may sense in a very real way
your loving presence and your healing touch
on our bodies and spirits.
Come to us, O Christ,
by way of the bread and the cup,
and by way of loving fellowship
with other members of your body,
to increase our faith, renew our courage,
and deepen our commitment
to you and your purposes in our world.
Come, O Lord, and give us your grace
to truly love one another.

HE DOES
ALL THINGS WELL

I proclaim your name
and shout your praises, my God.
You draw me into the crucible of conflict.
You test and try me in the valley of sorrow.
You allow me to taste the agony of affliction.
You even allow my peers to oppose and oppress me.
And then you use these very things
to purge and prepare me for your purposes.
So I shout your praises, O God,
for you do all things well,
and I know that you will love me forever.

IN A TIME
OF ECSTASY

Never before, O Lord, have I felt your nearness
as I have today.
It has been a burning-bush experience,
a Mount-of-Transfiguration episode in my life.
My every human sense and faculty was immersed
in the beauty and power of your presence.
I felt as if I might explode with joy.
O Jesus, you were so real, so precious, so close to me.
Why, my God, can't I always feel this way?
I know I must leave the mountaintop
to run your errands and serve your children
in the valley.
You must help me to understand and believe, O God,
that while my sense of your nearness
may dim or diminish,
the fact of your presence is forever secure.
You are always near.
You are with me and you will go before me
even amidst the tragedies and dark crises
that clutter my course through life.
Thank you, O Lord, for surprising me with joy.
May this ecstasy refresh and recharge
my life and my faith in you.
May it lead to deeper dedication to your purposes,
and bring joy to others who cross my path.

FROM GRIPING TO GRATITUDE

My loving God,
you have turned my griping into gratitude,
my screams of despair into proclamations of joy.
How can I help but explode with praises
and vow to spend eternity in giving thanks to you?
You are my hope and salvation,
my morning sun and evening star,
my shade in the desert heat,
my warmth in the cold of the night.
You are the Bread of Life,
and the life-giving springs
when my soul is parched and dry.
You are the answer to my agonizing questions,
the fulfillment of my deepest longings.
I am yours, O God, yours forever.
Make my life a perpetual offering of praise.

I PRAISE YOU

I praise you, O God.
As long as I have breath in my body,
I will praise you.
You created the earth and all that abides on it.
You can heal the wounds and mend the fractures
of this disjointed world.
You can break the bonds of humanity's obsessions
and pierce stupefaction with visions of truth.
You tenderly reach out to the oppressed
and reveal your concern for the lost and lonely.
You watch over your own,
and you love them and care for them.
I praise you, O God,
for truly you are a great God.

GROWING
OLDER

THE BONUS YEARS

I thank you, my God,
for these bonus years that you have added
to my full and active life on this earth.
Now I can do some of the things
I have always wanted but never had the time to do.
I seek to do those things, my Lord,
not only for my pleasure, but for your service.
I have letters to write,
people to see,
old friends to call,
ill and lonely people to comfort and cheer.
I thank you for whatever good health remains
and for your grace in enabling me
to carry out these projects.
Help me, my great God,
to use these days and years well,
to discover that my greatest joy
comes not in what I do for myself
but in what I do for others.
Even as I give of myself to the needs of others,
help me to find pleasure and fulfillment
in these bonus years before me.

ABOUT TO RETIRE

I am, O Lord, both regretting and rejoicing
as I face the prospect of leaving behind
the security and satisfaction of a task
that has been so much a part of my life.
I have invested so much of myself in my vocation
that leaving it behind is leaving behind
a large part of myself.
I feel at times as if my contribution to society
has been terminated, my significance diminished.
I feel both loss and uncertainty
as I am cut free from the daily discipline
of clock-punching and appointment-keeping,
of directing and being directed by others.
But I also rejoice for this blessed freedom.
I am freed from the constraints of deadlines,
from the need to excel or measure up
to a superior's demands and expectations.
I am freed to walk a different path
and pursue an unknown course.
I rejoice because I am not put away,
but simply freed to serve you, O God,
in ways not open to me before.
I thank you, God, that my life
does not end with retirement,
that in many ways this may be a beginning.
I will find exciting challenges
and renewed opportunities
to commit myself to you and your purposes.

CELEBRATING MARRIAGE

We are still married, our loving Lord,
and we are grateful,
to you above all, and to one another,
for the privilege and the pleasure
of these years together.
We know that it is not because of our charm
or ingenuity or determination,
but by your grace
that we are celebrating today.
There have been doubts and dry spells,
disagreements and misunderstandings.
There were even days when we seriously wondered
if it was worth it.
Whatever the reason, we stayed with it,
even through those rough times
when circumstances about us or within us
sought to drive a wedge between us.
We are grateful, dear God, that through it all
and with your gracious help
we have found a love
that is stronger and richer and more satisfying
than anything for which we dared to hope.
We're still married, and we thank you, our God.
We shall continue, in the days or years before us,
to live by your grace
and in obedience to your will.

ALWAYS YOUR SERVANT

I may not be able to serve you
with the energy and aggressiveness
of my youth, O loving God,
nor can I fill all those positions of responsibility
you once assigned to me,
but I rejoice in knowing
that I am always your servant.
Your commission is ever before me;
you will never rescind it.
Your power is available always,
and I am yours forever.
I may be serving in a smaller arena,
but the joy of serving is as great as ever, O God.
I am as important to you as I have ever been.
Assure me of my significance as your servant, O Lord,
and keep reminding me that, wherever I am,
there are people I can reach on your behalf,
proclaiming and demonstrating your love.
Empower me, guide me,
work out your will through me,
for I am always your servant.

GREETING EACH DAY WITH JOY

I may not be able to meet each day
in good health, my Lord,
but I can greet each day with joy.
You have canceled out my past failures;
you love me even in my weakness.
I praise you for your goodness
toward me these many years,
for your guarantee of life everlasting
in that glorious dimension
beyond this world in which I live.
I can do no less, Lord,
than to live each day to the full,
entrusting myself totally to your mercy
and expressing my joy in loving relationships
with those around me.
May the fire of your Spirit
burn brightly within me, Lord,
and may it cast light on the dark and lonely paths
of others who come my way.

MORE TIME
TO PRAY

I have more time to pray now, Lord,
for my dear children and their families,
for my friends,
for those who are ill or lonely,
for your oppressed and suffering children
throughout this world,
and for those servants who seek
to demonstrate to them
your love and care.
I may not be able to be on the front lines,
but I can and I do unite with those
who continue to show your concern for the multitudes
that have not yet embraced
your redeeming love.
Grant those who labor around the world
great joy and much power
as they reach out to communicate your love and grace
to people about them.
Continue to show me ways I might serve you
in the days or years I have before me.

GROWING OLD TOGETHER

How grateful we are, our Lord,
that we can grow old together!
There is a deep joy and abiding contentment
that we never quite realized
in the early years of our marriage.
There is less tension, less striving.
We are truly happy with each other.
We fit together,
knowing well and accepting fully
each other's strengths and weaknesses.
We thank you, our Lord, for keeping us
through the difficult years of our marriage,
for patiently teaching us how to love each other.
We are not yet at the end of our journey, O God.
There will still be battles to be fought,
wounds to be endured, victories to be won.
But our faith is stronger now—
and our love deeper—
as we seek to live out each day together with you.
Stay with us, Lord,
and continue to use us
as we grow old together.

WHEN WE GET LONELY

Sometimes we get lonely, Lord.
Our children, once so dependent on us,
do not need us any longer.
They have their own responsibilities—
and all the problems that go with them.
We cannot expect to be as important to them
as they were and are to us.
Bless them, Lord, and watch over them.
Now may we,
in our matured love for each other,
and in love exchanged with friends,
discover that fullness of love
which will overcome the emptiness and loneliness
that sometimes overwhelms us.
We thank you, God, for what our children
have meant and do mean to us.
Be with us in our absence from them.
Keep us busy with your purposes
and in sharing our love
with other lonely people
who come our way.

WHEN ONE OF US IS GONE

Because of your love and grace, O God,
we no longer fear the inevitable—
that day and that hour when we shall part company
with this world's pains and pleasures
to step into your perfect and total dimension for us.
We belong to you,
and nothing can separate us
from your eternal love.
There is something we do dread, O Lord.
It is that one of us will go before the other,
and that one will be left alone.
We have become so close
through our many years together
that it is difficult to contemplate
how we could possibly exist apart.
We are grateful for our years together,
the hours of struggle and defeat
as well as the times of joy and victory.
Teach us how to relish and use to the utmost
every day of our remaining years together.
Give to us the assurance, our God,
that your grace will continue to comfort and sustain
that one who is left behind
when one of us is gone.

AS THE YEARS GO BY

"Do not cast me off in the time of old age,"
said the psalmist,
"forsake me not when my strength is spent. . . .
They still bring forth fruit in old age,
they are ever full of sap and green."
The years are quickly going by, O God,
and while I know you will never forsake me,
I pray that I may continue to bring forth fruit,
that your Spirit within me may ever be young
and through me may reflect the effervescent joy,
the steadfast, rocklike faith
of your child and servant.
I pray that I may never be a burden
on my children or my friends,
but if such should happen,
let me be a blessed burden, even a happy burden,
that contributes joy and strength to their lives.
Help me, my Lord, to continue
to "proclaim thy might
to all the generations to come."
I thank you, O God, for the years behind me.
While they were filled with failures
to comprehend your will and serve in your purposes,
they were also full of your loving forgiveness
and reconciling grace.
I commit into your caring hands my remaining years.
May they be reflections of your love and glory.

WHEN THE HOUR GROWS LATE

My God, my Guide, my Master, and my Companion,
you have stayed close beside me
through more years than I care to count.
Through summers of joy and winters of discontent,
through springtimes of promise
and autumns of depression,
you have never left my side.
When I have fallen, you have picked me up.
When I recklessly walked the edge of ruin,
you were there to hold me back.
Even when I screamed in protest and rebelled,
your chastisement was gentle
and your love was constant.
Now it is getting late, O God,
and sometimes I feel resentful.
Forgive me for looking back, dear Lord,
except to glory in your presence and your care
throughout those perilous years.
I seek not to be younger in years,
but to be young and ever vital in spirit.
Grant, my God, that your eternal Spirit
may replenish the dry wells of my life,
that even though my bones may ache
and my activities diminish,
my life may be a spring of living water
to my sisters and brothers about me.

NATION
AND
WORLD

LOVE FOR COUNTRY

We love our country, O God.
The acquisition of our land
has not always been honorable.
Our treatment of minorities has been inexcusable.
Our selfish use of our land's resources is deplorable.
Yet there is so much beauty;
and where your precepts have been practiced,
light and liberty have pushed back the shades
of darkness and oppression.
We love our country, O God.
Teach us how to love its people—your people—
and how to share its rich treasures
with all your children,
whatever their race or creed or point of origin.
Protect us from our enemies, O God,
those enemies that threaten from within,
our apathy, our insensitivity,
our self-centeredness and bigotry.
Help us to keep our country, O God,
and to make it a secure and happy sanctuary
for all who dwell within it.

HEAL OUR LAND

Heal our land, O Lord.
We are not what we expected to be
or what you wanted us to be.
When we turn away from you,
we turn against one another.
There is poverty and oppression
and lawlessness and corruption.
Even many of our leaders,
while they recited worthy creeds,
have sought personal goals of wealth and power.
Give to us men and women
who will courageously seek and speak the truth
and who will dedicate their lives and their leadership
to the welfare of all the inhabitants
of our great country.
We are sick, O Lord, even unto death.
Heal our land, O Lord.

MY COUNTRY AND MY GOD

O Lord, this country has been my country
from the time of my birth.
It has been the recipient of your mercy and grace.
It has served your purposes
in acting for human rights in other parts of the world
and has contributed to the advancement
of your eternal kingdom all around the globe.
But this country has also been a breeding ground
for greed and selfishness, contributing to the suffering
of innocent people on this planet.
It has nurtured a brand of religiosity
that encourages self-gain and affluence
and shields its constituents from the horrors
that injustice and poverty inflict
upon your created children on other continents.
And I have been a part of all this, O God,
and have helped to make it this way.
I have relished my comfort and security
in this powerful, rich country—
in spite of the compelling challenges of your Word
to share in the suffering
of my sisters and brothers in other lands
and to share my good fortune with those in need.
Forgive me for my apathy and self-centeredness,
O God,
and grant me the grace to live and act as your servant
on behalf of the world's suffering multitudes.

CARE FOR
THE EARTH

Our world is beautiful and bountiful, O Lord.
It is because this is your world, your creation.
You have appointed and empowered us
to be your cocreators as well as your caretakers
of this beautiful planet.
We have harnessed great rivers
to provide for our daily needs,
and we have polluted them with our wastes.
We have turned barren lands into green parks,
and we have despoiled them with our carelessness.
We have carved up our valleys, stripped our forests,
depleted our soil, and even filled the very air
that we breathe with suffocating impurities.
We have selfishly possessed this earth for ourselves
and extracted from its vast treasures
more than was due us
and more than we needed to sustain us.
Appointed to create, we have chosen to abuse,
and even while we call ourselves your children,
we have vandalized and all but destroyed
the home you made for us.
We seek your forgiveness, O God,
and your wisdom to care for our earth
and to be faithful stewards over that
which you have entrusted to us.

139

THOSE WHO SERVE IN OUR WORLD

We pray today for those who serve in difficult places.
We offer our gratitude to you
for those in front-line positions
who are committed to demonstrating
and proclaiming your eternal love
in places where your Word and objectives
are not acclaimed or applauded.
We follow them with our prayers, O Lord,
that you would encourage and inspire,
comfort and sustain them in their service
to you and to your children.
Their successes are often not obvious
and cannot be measured by worldly standards.
There are pitfalls and precipices all about them.
Powerful people are hostile to them
and to you and your purposes.
But they are your children and your servants.
Grant them oases along their desert paths,
springs of water along steep and rocky trails,
and the joy and satisfaction of knowing
that they are close to your heart
and are walking obediently
in your course for their lives.
Grant, O Lord, that they be faithful to you,
and that we be faithful to them,
in praying for them, in loving and supporting them,
and in sharing with them your gracious gifts to us.

THE POOR AND OPPRESSED

It is easy, O God, to mouth my concern
for this world's oppressed and deprived peoples.
I pray that your love for me
will generate a genuine concern
for the suffering and dispossessed of the earth.
They are your children, Lord,
and they are my sisters and brothers.
They, too, constitute the body of Christ.
When one member suffers, the whole body suffers.
Even while I rejoice in your saving grace,
enable me to feel the hurt and to share in the pain
of other people.
Grant that I may be loving enough
to share with them your gifts to me
and wise enough to discover ways
to communicate to them
your eternal concern and love.

PEACE IN OUR WORLD

O Lord, you never guaranteed that we would have
perpetual peace in our disjointed world.
As we have used the fortunes of war for selfish ends,
so we often turn years of peace into opportunities
for self-service and personal gain.
But it need not be so, O God.
On behalf of the masses who have suffered
so terribly and for so long,
we dare to pray for world peace.
We pray, as well,
that a time of peace may be a time of opportunity
to demonstrate and to communicate true peace
to the scarred and wounded spirits of your children.
We pray once more
that swords will be beaten into plowshares,
that people of all races may commune
and share with and care for one another,
and that every human creature may learn about
the peace that is beyond understanding,
safe in the arms of a loving God.

FAITH IN A DISSOLVING WORLD

It is difficult, our loving God,
to demonstrate our joy and reflect your love
in a world that is falling apart.
Hatred and violence, dishonesty and disorder,
immortality and lawlessness run rampant
in this beautiful world you have created.
Hopelessness and despair haunt
the hearts of men and women.
While frightened people scurry about
for a place to hide
or concoct foolish gods to succor and sustain them,
we turn to you.
You are our Lord and our God.
We believe you to be present in our world
even when you seem so far away.
While we grasp for some sign of your presence,
some evidence of your reign over the universe,
teach us how to trust you through the Christ
who has revealed you to us,
to continue to communicate your saving love
amid the helplessness and despair
of a dissolving world.
Help us to believe that you are here
and through us are accomplishing
your purposes in our world today.
Strengthen and sustain our faith, O God,
that we might walk in obedience to you.

IN THE
EVENING

IT'S BEEN A GREAT DAY

It's been a great day, Lord!
When I least expected it, I met you.
Forgive me for not anticipating your presence
in the people who cross my path.
Thank you for touching me with loving concern
in spite of my apathy and doubt,
for revealing yourself even through the gentle words
and actions of that one who,
though he didn't realize it,
lifted me out of my depression and self-pity
and put hope and joy into my life again.
Bless him, O God.
And make me that kind of person who will reflect
your joy in the midst of this world's loneliness
and communicate your love and peace
to anxious, weary, confused, unhappy,
hate-filled hearts about me.
Then tomorrow will also be a great day,
and I will celebrate your presence wherever I go.

I TRIED
TO RUN AWAY

Dear Jesus,
I know that you never left me today,
but I'm afraid I tried to run away from you.
Instead of following you,
I decided to lead the way.
I took things into my own hands,
and I ended up hurting those I wanted to help.
I meant well, Lord, but I performed so poorly.
O God, forgive me,
and make even out of the ashes of my errors
something that will be pleasing to you.
Teach me how to rest in your will,
to wait for your guidance,
and to speak and act in gentleness and love,
whatever the circumstances or difficulties
of each day.

YOU NEVER LEFT MY SIDE

I thank you, my loving God,
because, whether I win or lose,
I am secure in my relationship to you.
You may not have approved
of everything I did today,
but you stayed with me and never left my side.
I didn't see you around every corner.
There were long hours during which
I never even thought about you.
And yet I knew you were close to me.
Thank you, Lord,
for the sweet assurance that you love me,
that I belong to you,
that you will never let me go.
I do not fear the night or the morrow.
Even if tomorrow never comes,
I rest in the arms of your forgiving love,
for I am yours forever.

THANK YOU
FOR THE NIGHT

Thank you for the night, dear Lord,
for the rest and peace displacing
the panic and frustrations of the day.
Thank you for the time to mend life's ragged edges
and to refocus the heart and mind
on things that are truly important.
And thank you for your word of forgiveness,
for the assurance of your love,
and for the knowledge that, as I rest my weary body,
I rest my spirit in your tender care.
Thank you, God,
that even before I lapse into unconsciousness,
I can discover anew my identity as your child,
and should I awaken to the morrow,
I will begin a new day of challenge and opportunity
as your child and your servant.
Thank you, Lord.

WHEN I
AM LONELY

I am lonely, Lord.
It is not the absence of people
that causes my complaint;
they have bustled by me throughout the day.
It is the absence of love and concern.
They would pause momentarily if they could use me.
They were even willing at times to abuse me.
Not one, Lord, not one was honestly concerned
about my feelings or my needs.
Forgive me, Lord, for wallowing in self-pity.
You have also walked the path of loneliness
and found comfort in the love of our Father.
It is true, O Lord, that even while I am lonely,
I am never alone.
I commit myself to your loving care this night,
and pray that on the morrow
I may not waste pity on myself,
but seek to express it in valid terms of loving concern
for those equally lonely people
who bustle by me throughout the day.

PICK UP
THE PIECES

It has been one of those days, O Lord,
that I wish had never happened.
I've been zapped, squashed, beaten down.
It wasn't at all like the kind of victorious living
I had anticipated would be my lot as your servant.
I'm sorry, Lord, that I am so inept,
so foolish and clumsy
in my attempts to carry out your purposes.
There are some days when nothing seems to work,
when everything I touch falls apart,
when I could just as well have stayed in bed.
May I entrust even these days
into your hands, O God?
Is it possible that you can make something
out of them that I could not?
I submit to you not victories, but ashes.
Pick up the broken pieces of this day, O Lord,
and rework them into something
of value and significance.
Let me rest in the peace of your loving pardon,
and, if it be your will,
let me rise to a new day with courage and confidence.

THE DAY IS OVER

The day is over, O God,
and I commit its failures as well as its successes
into your hands.
I rejoice in your tender care
and celebrate your loving presence.
I pray that you will
heal the wounds of those I have hurt
and enrich the lives of those I have helped.
I place in your care those I love the most
and those through whom you ministered to me today.
Bless them and keep them and fill their lives with joy.
I pray that you may somehow reach those
I couldn't love or make to feel my love,
that others of your faithful servants
may relate your concern for them.
Grant that I may truly learn
how to love as you love me
and to demonstrate that love
to lonely, despairing people in my path.
This day is over, O God,
with its blessings and conflicts and disappointments.
If it be within your will, grant me another day,
and help me to live it within your plan for my life.

CONTEMPORARY
PSALMS

PSALM 8

O God,
   how full of wonder and splendor you are!

I see the reflections of your beauty
   and hear the sounds of your majesty
      wherever I turn.
Even the babbling of babes
   and the laughter of children
      spell out your name in indefinable syllables.

When I gaze into star-studded skies
   and attempt to comprehend the vast distances,
I contemplate in utter amazement
   my Creator's concern for me.
I am dumbfounded that you
   should care personally about me.

And yet you have made me in your image.
You have called me your child.
You have ordained me as your priest
   and chosen me to be your servant.
You have assigned to me
   the fantastic responsibility
      of carrying on your creative activity.

O God,
   how full of wonder and splendor you are!

PSALM 13

O God, sometimes you seem so far away.
I cannot in this moment sense your presence
   or feel your power.

The darkness about me is stifling.
This depression is suffocating.
How long, O God, do I have to live in this void?
O God, how long?

Break into this black night, O God;
   fill in this vast emptiness.
Enter into my conflict
   lest I fall never to rise again.

I continue to trust in your ever-present love.
I shall again discover true joy
   in my relationship to you.
I will proclaim your praises, my Lord,
   for you will never let me go.

PSALM 23

The Lord is my constant companion.
There is no need that he cannot fulfill.
Whether his course for me points
    to the mountaintops of glorious ecstasy
    or to the valleys of human suffering,
  he is by my side,
  he is ever present with me.
He is close beside me
    when I tread the dark streets of danger,
    and even when I flirt with death itself,
  he will not leave me.
When the pain is severe,
  he is near to comfort.
When the burden is heavy,
  he is there to lean upon.
When depression darkens my soul,
  he touches me with eternal joy.
When I feel empty and alone,
  he fills the aching vacuum with his power.
My security is in his promise
    to be near to me always,
  and in the knowledge
    that he will never let me go.

PSALM 33

God is here—let's celebrate!
With song and with dance,
    with stringed instruments and brass,
    with cymbals and drums,
  let us express ecstatic joy in God's presence.
Let us celebrate with the old songs of praise.
Let us also create new songs
  that portray the eternal love of our God.

He did create this world.
He continues to permeate it with his love.
Even among its frustrated and unbelieving children,
  he constantly carries out his purposes.
His plans for his world and its inhabitants
  are not obliterated by the foolishness of men.
His truth is not blotted out by the lethargy or lies
  of his apathetic creatures.
He continues to reign and to reveal himself to us.

And God continues to create and to renew
  the world about us.
He does this through those who relate to him,
  who rely on his ever-present love.
He delivers his children from the fear of death
  and through them gives life to this world.
God's love is sure and everlasting.
Hearts open to his love are filled with joy.
They truly find cause for celebration.

PSALM 111

My heart is full today.
I am so grateful
    for all that God has done for me.
I need but crawl out of my corner
        of depression and self-pity
    and look around me to see
        how great my God is.
I cannot see him,
    but I can see the works of his hands.
He is a merciful and loving God.
How tenderly he deals with those
    whose hearts are open to him!
He is a righteous and faithful God.
His promises and precepts are forever.
He is a majestic and powerful God.
He created me and sustains me day by day.
He is a forgiving God.
He takes me back to his loving heart
    when I go astray.
He is in this world today.
And those who recognize and accept his presence
    are building on foundations
        that are eternally secure.
How grateful I am to my God today!

PSALM 126

Let us begin this day by rejoicing!
Let us acknowledge our Lord's love and concern
   and allow our bodies to break forth
     into happy hilarity!
Let us give our nerves and muscles
   the healthy exercise of laughter!
The Lord has done such wonderful things for us;
   let us be glad!

The day before us is uncertain.
We know not what we will encounter on our way.
While we rejoice with those who rejoice,
   we shall also weep with those who suffer.
While we may be surprised by ecstasy,
   we may also pass through corridors of darkness.
Wherever we go, we go forth as children and servants
     of the living God,
   and we go forth to touch the lives of men and
      women
    with his healing love.
Let us begin this day with rejoicing,
   and return to our homes with gladness!

Leslie F. Brandt is a leading author of books of prayer, meditation, and devotion. This volume is an expanded and revised edition of his earlier *Book of Christian Prayer,* designed for personal, family, and group use. In *Growing Together* he and his wife Edith published prayers for married couples. Brandt is best known for his paraphrases of the Psalms and other portions of the Scriptures. Among his well-known books are *Psalms/Now, Good Lord, Where Are You?, Epistles/Now, Prophets/Now,* and *Jesus/Now.*

Pastor Brandt served as a missionary in China and as pastor of congregations in Minnesota, North Dakota, and California. He continues his ministry of preaching, writing, and speaking in Hawaii.